DATE DUE

THE SUN

A TRUE BOOK

by

Allison Lassieur

Children's Press®

A Division of Grolier Publishing

New York London Hong Kong Sydney
Danbury, Connecticut

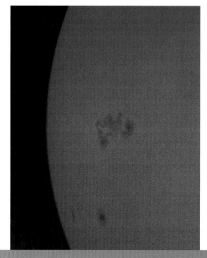

Content Consultant
Peter Goodwin
*Kent School
Kent, CT*

The photograph on the cover shows sunspots near the center of the Sun. The photograph on the title page shows a beautiful sunset.

The dark spots on this photograph of the Sun are called sunspots. They are caused by dark gases that swirl around the Sun.

Visit Children's Press® on the Internet at:
http://publishing.grolier.com

Library of Congress Cataloging-in-Publication Data

Lassieur, Allison
   The Sun / by Allison Lassieur.
      p. cm. — (A true book)
   Includes bibliographical references and index.
   Summary: Describes how the Sun is formed, what it is made of, old ideas about it, and how the Sun affects Earth.
    ISBN: 0-516-22002-0 (lib. bdg.)   0-516-27188-1 (pbk.)
   Sun—Juvenile literature. [1. Sun.] I. Title. II. Series

QB521.5.L38 2000   99-055982
523.7—dc21

Contents

Long ago, people worshiped the Sun. Today, we still appreciate its power and beauty.

The Sun in History

People have always under-stood that the Sun has amazing power. Long ago, there was no way for people to study the Sun. Instead, they worshiped it as a god. In many countries, people told stories that explained why the Sun moves across the sky each day.

This ancient Egyptian scroll shows Ra, the Sun god, riding in his Sun boat. The god Seth is spearing Ra's enemy, the serpent Apophis.

The ancient Greeks believed that the Sun god Helios drove a chariot across the sky. The Chinese thought that a huge dragon chased the Sun through the heavens. The Egyptians believed their sun god Ra put the Sun in his boat and carried it across the sky.

Sunny Structures

Some ancient people built special observatories to watch the Sun. Most scientists believe that the circle of large rocks at Stonehenge in England were used to record the movements of the Sun, Moon, and stars.

On Midsummer Day, the sun rises between the last two columns of the Temple of Amon in Egypt (top).

A group of early Native Americans built a huge wheel of stones in what is now Wyoming. It is called the Big Horn Medicine Wheel (bottom). Some people think that it was built to line up with the Sun at certain times of the year.

New Ideas

As time went on, people wanted to know more about the Sun. One early scientist thought the Sun was only 12 inches (30 centimeters) across. Another thought the Sun was about 35 miles (56 kilometers) wide and 4,000 miles (6,440 km) away from Earth. Today we know that the

The Sun looks small because it is far away. In reality, the Sun is about 100 times wider than our planet.

Sun is about 100 times wider than Earth. It is 865,000 miles (1,392,000 km) across and about 92 million miles (148 million km) away.

Claudius Ptolemaeus, also called Ptolemy, believed that the Sun and the other planets revolved around Earth.

An ancient Greek scientist named Claudius Ptolemaeus thought that Earth was at the center of the Universe. He said that the Sun circled around Earth. For almost 2,000 years, most people thought Ptolemaeus was right.

Then, in the 1500s, a scientist named Nicolaus Copernicus suggested that Earth and the other planets move around the Sun. A few years later, another scientist named Galileo Galilei

The Italian scientist Galileo Galilei built this telescope to study the night sky.

used a new invention called a telescope to prove that Copernicus was right. Today we know that Earth is one of nine planets that orbit the Sun.

What Is the Sun?

Our Sun is a star—a huge ball of hot glowing gases. The planets in our solar system orbit the Sun because it pulls on them with a force called gravity. All objects in space have some gravity. The bigger an object is, the more gravity it has. The Sun's tug is so strong because

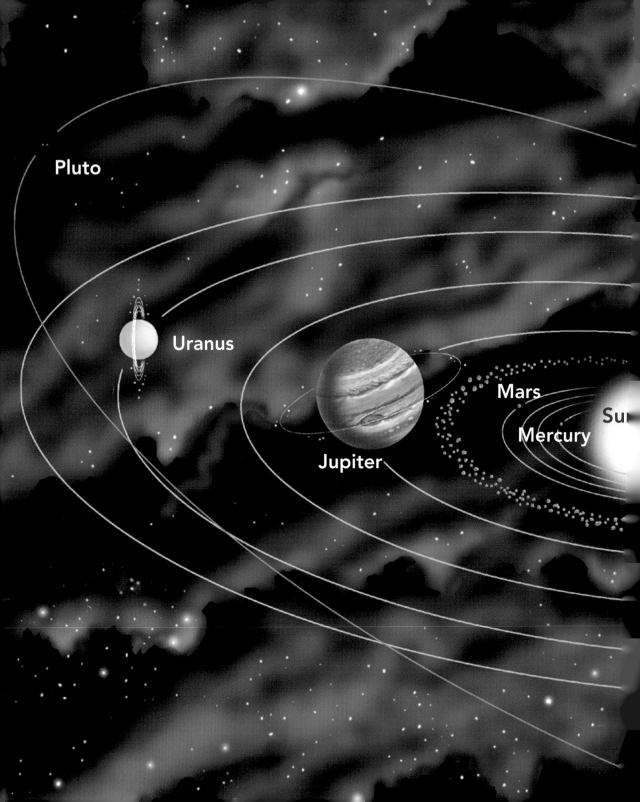

The Solar System

Venus

Moon

Earth

Asteroid Belt

Saturn

Neptune

it is much larger than any of the planets.

The planets Mercury and Venus are closer to the Sun than Earth is. The planets Mars, Jupiter, Saturn, Uranus, Neptune, and Pluto are all farther from the Sun than Earth is. Planets close to the Sun are much warmer than planets far from the Sun. The Sun's pull holds Earth in an orbit that keeps the planet's temperature just right for living things.

Warm sunlight shines through forests and provides the energy plants need to grow. Life thrives on Earth because its orbit is just the right distance from the Sun.

Our Sun looks larger than the stars in the night sky, but it is really an average-sized star.

There are billions and billions of stars in the universe. Compared to most stars, our Sun is tiny. It looks so big and bright to you because it is the closest star to Earth.

When you see the Sun in the sky, it seems calm and steady. But actually it is always changing. A stream of material called the solar wind constantly shoots out from the Sun. Solar wind flies all the way past the

This view of the solar wind was sent to Earth by a spacecraft orbiting to the Sun.

planets in our solar system. The solar wind zooms through space about 250 miles (400 km) a second. At that speed, it takes about 4 to 5 days for the solar wind to reach Earth.

When solar wind hits Earth's atmosphere, people near the North and South Poles sometimes see colorful lights in the sky. The northern lights are called the aurora borealis. The southern

The northern lights are among of the world's most spectacular natural displays.

lights are called the aurora australis.

Solar wind is really hot. It is about 1 million degrees Fahrenheit (555,600 degrees Celsius). Believe it or not, the center of the Sun is much hotter than that. It is hard to imagine something that hot!

Mysteries of the Sun

We expect to see the Sun rise every morning and set every night, but sometimes strange things happen. Even when there are no clouds in the sky, the Sun may disappear in the middle of the day. This is called a solar eclipse. During a solar eclipse, the Moon moves

During a total solar eclipse, the Moon moves between Earth and the Sun.

between Earth and the Sun and blocks the Sun's light for a short time.

Sunspots (above) might look small, but most are bigger than our entire planet. This photograph (left) shows what a sunspot looks like close up.

The Sun is sometimes covered with dark spots called sunspots. Sunspots look dark because they are cooler than the gases around them. The number of sunspots increases and then decreases until finally they disappear for a while. The whole process takes about 11 years.

Solar flares are huge bursts of energy that explode on the Sun's surface near sunspots. They are so powerful that

Solar flares can explode hundreds of miles above the Sun's surface.

they can hurl energy from the Sun all the way to Earth in 8 minutes. When all this energy is let loose in space, it causes solar storms.

Solar storms hit Earth often, but they cannot always be seen or felt by humans. Sometimes they are so strong that they cause electrical power to go out.

Earth spins like a top as it travels around the Sun. It takes 365 1/4 days to make its journey around the Sun. It takes 24 hours to spin around once. As the Earth turns, the side of the planet you are on turns away from the Sun in the afternoon and gets dark at night. When it is nighttime where you live, the Sun is rising over countries and oceans on the opposite side of Earth. At night, you see the Sun's light reflected on the Moon.

Night

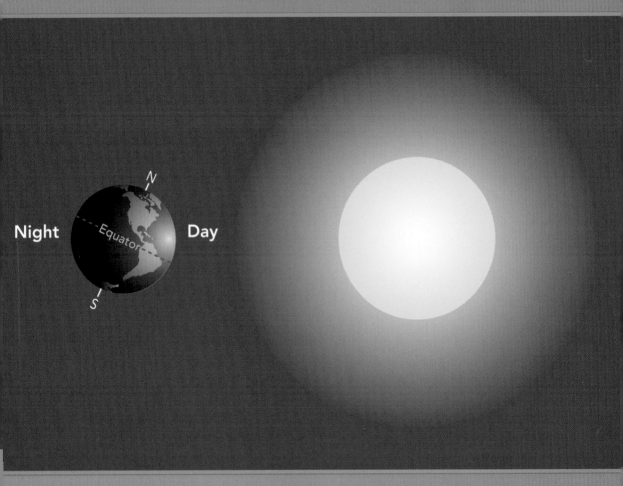

Night   N   Equator   Day   S

Earth spins as it orbits the Sun. As our planet spins, different areas of the planet face the Sun. When it is night, the part of Earth you are on faces away from the Sun.

Studying the Sun

Scientists can't look directly at the Sun. It is so bright that it could blind them. That is why scientists use special telescopes to study the Sun. They are called solar telescopes. A solar telescope protects a person's eyes by reducing the amount of light it lets through.

Solar telescopes are built to protect a person's eyes from the blinding light of the Sun.

Scientists have built huge solar telescopes at several places on Earth so they can watch the Sun 24 hours a day. When it is night at Big Bear Solar Observatory in California, the Udaipur Solar Observatory in western India is facing the Sun.

Scientists also study the Sun from space. In 1995, a group of scientists from the United States and Europe worked together to send the

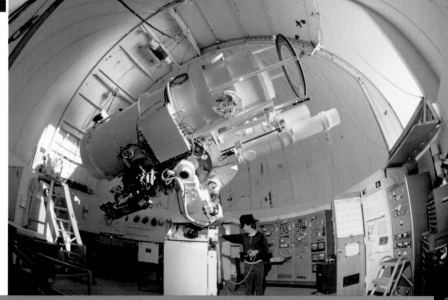

The Big Bear Solar Observatory sits in the middle of Big Bear Lake in California (top). The cloudless skies and clear air over Big Bear Lake, make the area an excellent place to observe the Sun (bottom).

The SOHO satellite sits on top of the huge Atlas rocket before its launch into space.

Solar and Heliospheric Observatory (SOHO) into orbit around the Sun. The Sun never sets on SOHO's telescope. It always has a view of the Sun.

How the Sun Affects Earth

Energy from the Sun causes weather and seasons. When the Sun's rays hit the ground, they warm it. The warm ground heats the air above it. As the air heats, it rises and makes wind.

When the air close to the ground heats, it rises. As it comes into contact with cooler air, wind forms.

The Sun also warms the water on Earth. Some of the warm water turns into a gas and rises into the air. When the

Clouds might look solid, but they are really made of the gas that forms when liquid water evaporates.

gas cools off, it forms clouds. Sometimes the gases that make up clouds fall back to Earth as rain, snow, hail, or sleet.

Green plants turn the Sun's energy into food (above). When an animal eats a green plant (right), it gets the energy that originally came from the Sun.

Without the Sun, Earth would be a cold, black rock in space. There would be no life on Earth at all. All the energy that living things need to grow comes from the Sun. Green plants soak up the Sun's energy and turn it into food. When animals eat the plants, they change the Sun's energy into energy their bodies can use. When meat-eating animals eat the plant-eating animals, the energy is passed on.

The lettuce and tomato on a hamburger are filled with energy from the Sun—and so is the meat.

The next time you eat a hamburger with lettuce and tomato, think about what you are putting in your mouth. You are really getting some of the Sun's energy. Yum!

To Find Out More

These places are great for more information about the Sun and the planets.

Books

Asimov, Isaac. **The Sun and Its Secrets.** Gareth Stevens Publishing, 1994.

Bourgeois, Paulette and Bill Slavin. **The Sun.** Kids Can Press, 1997.

Daily, Robert. **The Sun.** Franklin Watts, 1994.

Daley, Michael J. and Buckley Smith. **Amazing Sun Fun Activities.** McGraw-Hill, 1998.

Daley, Michael. **Sun Fun.** McGraw-Hill, 1997.

Estalella, Robert. **Our Star: The Sun.** Barrons Juveniles, 1993.

Taylor, Peter O. and Nancy L. Hendrickson. **Beginner's Guide to the Sun.** Kalmbach Publishing Company, 1996.

Vogt, Gregory L. **The Sun.** Milbrook, 1996.

💡 Organizations and Online Sites

National Aeronautics and Space Administration (NASA)
http://www.nasa.gov

This site has information about every part of space travel, from moon missions to life on the space shuttle.

National Air and Space Museum
Smithsonian Institution
601 Independence Ave. SW
Washington, DC 20560
http://www.nasm.si.edu/

Visit the museum's great website for information about exhibits and special programs.

The Nine Planets
http://seds.lpl.arizona.edu/ nineplanets/nineplanets/

Jump aboard a spaceship and tour the solar system on this website.

Solar Folklore
http://solar-center. stanford.edu/folklore/ folklore.html

Stories about the Sun from around the world are only a click away at this site.

Important Words

atmosphere the layer of gases that surrounds a planet

eclipse when the view of a planet, moon, or star is blocked

energy the ability to do work

gravity a force that pulls objects toward one another

observatory a building with equipment that scientists can use to study objects in the sky

orbit to move around an object

solar system all the objects that orbit around the Sun

solar wind a stream of dust that constantly shoots off the Sun

telescope an instrument that makes far-away objects look closer

Index

Meet the Author

Allison Lassieur is the author of more than a dozen children's books about health, history, world cultures, current events, and American Indians. She has also written articles for such magazines as *Disney Adventures*, *Scholastic News*, *Highlights for Children*, and *National Geographic World*.

When Ms. Lassieur is not writing, she enjoys reading, playing with her spinning wheel, and participating in historical reenactments.